ALL WE NEED IS LOVE

ALL WE NEED IS LOVE

Thoughts for the Millennium

Margaret Livingston-Fairley

The Book Guild Ltd
Sussex, England

The Book Guild Ltd.
25 High Street,
Lewes, Sussex

First published 2000
© Margaret Livingston-Fairley 2000
© Illustrations Anne Wilding 2000

Set in Bembo
Typesetting by
Acorn Bookwork, Salisbury, Wiltshire

Printed in Great Britain by
Bookcraft (Bath) Ltd, Avon

A catalogue record for this book is
available from the British Library

ISBN 1 85776 496 X

Dedicated, firstly, to my remarkable mother who devoted her whole life so lovingly to her family and taught us, by her example, how to love. Secondly, to my father who encouraged us to form our own opinions and never accept those of others without question. By example, he taught us how to discuss: his theory being that children may be too young to take part in conversation but never too young to listen.

★

And prizing more than Plato, things I learned
At that best Academe, a mother's knee.

J.R. Lowell

I would like to thank Anne Wilding of The Elm Tree Gallery, Woolpit, Bury St Edmunds, Suffolk, for her beautiful illustrations which contribute so much to my book.

ACKNOWLEDGEMENTS

The author has endeavoured to trace all copyright holders for the quotations in this anthology and apologises for any omissions, which will be rectified in future editions.

Virginia M. Axline
Quotation from *Dibs in Search of Self*. (Houghton Mifflin Co.)

Henry Drummond
Quotation from *The Greatest Thing in the World*. (Roger Schlesinger)

Coretta Scott King
The Words of Martin Luther King reprinted with kind permission of Robson Books Ltd.

Kahlil Gibran
Speak to us of Work and *Speak to us of Love* are from *The Prophet*. (William Heinemann)

The Song of the Flower and *The Life of Love* are from *Tears and Laughter*. (Carol Publishing Group, New York)

Max Ehrmann
Quotations from *The Desiderata of Happiness*. Published by Blue Mountain Arts Inc., Boulder, Colorado, USA 80306
Copyright 1948 by Bertha K. Ehrmann. All rights reserved. Reprinted by permission Robert L. Bell, Melrose, Ma. USA 02176.

Rabindranath Tagore
Quotations are from *Poems and Plays*. The publisher is Macmillan. Reprinted by permission Visva-Bharti University Calcutta 700 017, India. (Founded by R. Tagore)

Quotations from *The Return of Arthur Conan Doyle* edited by Ian Cooke and *Heal Thyself* are reprinted with kind permission from The White Eagle Publishing Trust at New Lands, Liss, Hampshire, GU33 7HY.

INTRODUCTION

This anthology on love, together with my own observations on the subject, were started many years ago when I lived with my husband on the edge of the Sahara. He worked for an oil company and I taught in the oil company school. There were children from all over the world. They belonged to all religions and worked and played together, most of the time, with love and friendliness. We adults have so much to learn from children.

The quietness and peacefulness of the desert are indescribable and it is an ideal place to think and reflect. Things that were once so important become "just trivia" and life takes on a completely new meaning.

Irongray Church Dumfries

The Routin' Brig, Irongray, Dumfries

All We Need Is Love

Duty without love, makes a person an annoyance;
Responsibility without love, makes a person ruthless;
Justice without love, makes a person hard;
Intelligence without love, makes a person cunning;
Kindness without love, makes a person a hypocrite;
Honour without love, makes a person arrogant;
Possession without love, makes a person avaricious;
Faith without love, makes a person fanatical;
A life without love, is meaningless.

Love is the greatest thing in the world.

Love, the true love that seeks for nought
The love that Christ and Buddah brought,
Comes like a wind, we know not whence,
But comes not from the world of sense.

★

Love – love life, love all the blessings that are yours,
Live to love – love to live.

★

You live that you may learn to love,
You love that you may learn to live,
No other lesson is required of man.

★

Love is kind and suffers long,
Love is meek and thinks no wrong,
Love than death itself's more strong,
Therefore, give us love.

The spectrum of love has nine ingredients and these make up the supreme gift – the stature of the perfect man no matter what his colour, religion or philosophy happen to be.

Patience	–	love suffereth long.
Kindness	–	and is kind.
Generosity	–	love envieth not.
Humility	–	love vaunteth not itself, is not puffed up.
Courtesy	–	doth not behave itself unseemly.
Unselfishness	–	seeketh not her own.
Good Temper	–	is not easily provoked.
Guilelessness	–	thinketh no evil.
Sincerity	–	rejoiceth not in iniquity but rejoiceth in the truth.

Henry Drummond

Martin Luther King said:

Love is the only force capable of transforming an enemy into a friend

★

Clear and penetrating is the eye of love. Therefore, it sees no faults. When love has purged your sights then you would see nothing at all unworthy of your love. Only a love-shorn faulty eye is ever busy finding faults. Whatever faults it finds are only its own faults.

Mikhail Naimy

★

Love, truth and the courage to do what is right should be our own guideposts on this lifelong journey.

★

Every injustice in the world today can be traced to a lack of love.

★

We should all aim to love the well-being of other persons as we love our own well-being. It is so easy to love loveable people – infinitely more difficult to love the unloveable. This is when real love is tested. How can we be expected to love those who, through their insensitive behaviour, remove all peace and dignity from life – even from people in their own homes? We can only pray that one day we shall be able to do so. We are still in the bottom class of the nursery school as far as "loving" is concerned.

4

How difficult is the path of love. I will try to walk a blameless path – but how I need your help!

★

Some time ago, I read the lovely story of Mr Gordon Lindsay, a Scottish actuary, who has chosen to live out his last years in paradise – in Swaziland – not as an expatriate drinking sundowners at all white clubs and reminiscing about colonial times, but as the adopted subject of a Swazi chief and honorary father to a Swazi native.

Gordon's fascination with Africa began when he happened to study the old accounts of a Caribbean sugar estate. The slaves were valued at £160 but one entry read: 'Sammy, in poor health – £20.' 'I felt when I cross over to the next world I would like to be able to look Sammy in the face.'

He has chosen to live quietly with the Swazi family he befriended years ago. David Hiatshwayo, then only a student, is now married with a son and has followed the Swazi custom of caring for elders by inviting Gordon to move in. Their son, Ntumelo, feels very close to Gordon and sees nothing odd in having a white, kilted grandfather.

'Colour melts away', says David. 'When one loves, colour or creed are totally unimportant.'

★

One word keep for me in thy silence, O world, when I am dead, "I have loved".

Rabindranath Tagore

★

5

Most ambitious people seek success for one reason only – the power it gives them over others. All social, national and international problems can only be solved by love; by love finding expression in forbearance, patience, service – in a word, by man living in fellowship with his neighbour, no matter what his colour or creed.

★

Ordinary people are tired of power-seeking leaders who have caused untold misery down the centuries to the present time.
They yearn for power and it is still one of the tragedies of human history that the "children of darkness" are more determined and zealous than the "children of light".

Martin Luther King

★

The absence of love in childhood creates incredible problems and the classic story of Dibs illustrates admirably the depth of suffering in children denied love by parents.

Dibs was a little boy born to wealthy, career-minded parents who had not planned on having a family. There was no love in his life at all and at the age of five he was sent to a therapist to whom the mother wrote the following: 'It soon became obvious that Dibs was abnormal. It is bad enough to have a child, but to have a mentally handicapped one is really more than we can bear. We were ashamed – we were humiliated. There had never been anything like this in either of our families... All our values had been slanted heavily in the direction of intelligence – fine, precise, noteworthy, intellectual achievement.'

Among the pediatricians who tried in vain to diagnose the nature of Dibs's problems, one summed up with the comment, 'He's a strange one... Who knows? Brain-damaged? Who can get close enough to find out how he ticks?'

Fortunately, someone did get close enough and was able, through her loving insight, delicate skill and infinite patience to rescue him from the fate of a mental hospital which was under consideration. The therapist who perceived intuitively the nature of the frustrations from which Dibs was suffering, helped the child to find himself and to recover the sanity he so nearly lost. Instead of entering a mental hospital, he became a brilliant young student of unusual sensitivity, courage and consideration for others. His IQ was rated at 160 and at the age of 15 he was described as having a 'social and spiritual development beyond that of many adults'.

Dibs is by Virginia M. Axline.

★

Dibs was a lucky man. How many lives are destroyed by lack of love in childhood? Love is as necessary to the development of the child as are food and water. We all, each one of us, need to be loved – in that way we burst forth into bud and eventually bloom. There is no worse fate for man than to live and grow old unloved and unloving.

★

I know nothing sadder than the "lack-lustre" eyes in a child's face.

Michael Quoist

★

The world's children deserve to be loved and nurtured. If we ignore this duty as adults we are ignoring the future of the human race. We are already witnessing incredible acts of violence and abuse in societies all over the world carried out by children from a variety of backgrounds. There is a disturbing lack of caring and sensitivity towards others and alarm bells ought to be ringing.

One little nine-year-old boy said to me, 'Margaret, I have both a mother and a father but neither can look after me. I think I must be the unluckiest boy in the whole world. Sometimes I just want to die and live with Jesus.'

A beautiful, articulate little boy who asks only to be wanted and loved. Can the adult world be surprised if he, and thousands like him, grows up insensitive, aggressive and unaware? I think not.

When one quietly considers the state of the world today one feels religions, any religion, have little to be proud of. There is hatred and bitterness all over the place with religion as its basis – everyone fighting over who "owns" God. I personally feel that 60 years ago, when I was a child, people were more loving, aware and generally more sensitive than they appear to be today. This being so, what have religion and philosophy been doing for the past 60 years?

A little nine-year-old Moslem girl came crying to me at the beginning of a lesson that a classmate – a Hindu girl – told her that Allah was "rubbish". She was obviously deeply upset and I decided I had a marvellous opportunity to discuss religion in a simple way with the whole class of 16 children – from nine different countries. I used the following verse from an Indian folk song to illustrate my points, which were accepted by the children and calm returned to the class. Children accept, more readily than adults, that people from other cultures also have something valid to say:

> Into the bosom of one great sea,
> Flow streams that come from hills on every side.
> Their names are various as their springs
> And thus in every land do men bow down
> To one great God, though known by many names.

It is up to parents and teachers, through discussion and example, to make sure that our young are adequately educated in this direction. The most important thing parents can give their children is time – and it costs absolutely nothing. Our young must be taught to love – this being the most important lesson in life. They must be taught to love every member of the human family irrespective of class, colour, creed or handicap; animal and bird, tree and flower – in fact every living thing on our planet.

Conversation in the home is so important and with this "tool" parents can actually mould a child's character for good or evil. As a child, brought up in the 30s when life was incredibly hard for everyone, I remember a great shortage of money everywhere but I also remember the richness of home life and the conversation that took place when people visited just to sit, have a drink and discuss. Children may have been seen and not heard but I can still recapture conversations I heard in my home. I realised when I was older that I was listening to very intelligent people discussing not only world problems, but the dreadful problems of poverty in our inner cities where mothers worked literally to buy shoes for their children and the ineffectiveness of politicians to do anything for them.

I remember unions being discussed and my father saying angrily, 'Mark my words – one day those unions will destroy British Industry'.

What foresight and from a very caring socialist too. He could foresee the great power struggle that would ensue one day which would not be in the interests of ordinary union members or this country.

As children we were taught to love and care about others. My father told us on one occasion that the cardinal sin was to do something to harm another human being. I remember asking, 'What does "cardinal" mean, Daddy?'

We were fortunate to have Meggie, the girl next door, who suffered from Down's syndrome. She spent a great deal of her time with us as children and crawled through a hole in the fence to visit. She came to school with us and the teachers were happy to have her work at her own pace.

Having Meggie share our school experience taught us, once again at an early age, to love and respect others no matter what their circumstances or handicap. Meggie was not shut away in a special school – there were very few at that time – but educated in a normal situation and as a result her achievements for someone so handicapped were incredible. She could read fluently and do basic arithmetic. She could travel nine miles by bus to do her mother's shopping and only felt upset when at the age of eleven she had to part company with her school friends and go to a special unit adjoining the local mental hospital. Her mother became ill with arthritis and when her father died she looked after her mother until she also died. After her mother's death she had to go into a home.

Once again conversations between my mother and Meggie's come to mind. Meggie's mother agonised over her future when she died. I can still hear my mother comforting her and assuring her that all would be well. Parents of handicapped children have so much to cope with and the future that awaits their beloved children when they are not around to care for them is a worry that is always with them.

I feel, with hindsight, that conversation had an incredible influence on me and I learnt so much from it at a very early, impressionable age. If we reflect for a moment we will realise that the wrong sort of conversation must also have a profound effect on the development of children who absorb everything, including atmospheres, like pieces of blotting paper.

Parents ought to create a daily "chat" time with their children listening and "hearing" what they have to say. They may be young but they also have a story to tell and in their own way do a "hard day's work" at school. Children are missing out on something quite precious if they rush to school in the morning, return home to an empty house or to parents who are too tired, or simply can't be bothered, to communicate with them. They have tea while they watch as much television as possible.

School is a guide to children but the real lasting influence for good or evil rests with parents. Money and material things have nothing to do with this – it is the quality of the parenting that sets the tone. Time is what children need – time to walk, talk and generally be with them as companions and friends as well as parents. The early years are the most impressionable and one can well understand the Jesuits' promise – 'Give me a child until he is seven and I will show you the man'. If children are deprived of love and understanding in the early years they rarely recover. A relative in my family is a prison secretary and she told me that, without exception, every prisoner had suffered a disturbed background.

★

I journeyed from university to
university, and I saw everywhere the
past rebuilt before the eyes of
young men and young women –
Egypt, Greece, Rome; language,
architecture, laws – saw the earth and
sky explained, and the habits of body –
Everywhere chairs of this and that,
largely endowed.
But nowhere saw I a chair of the
human heart.

Max Ehrmann

Confucius had a great deal to say about the role of the family and elders in general. His teaching is just as valid today as it was 2,500 years ago. As I recall, when Confucius was exiled to a northern Chinese state he became a public prosecutor. On one occasion a father brought his son to him for punishment. Confucius promptly put both father and son in prison, much to the anger of the prince of that particular state and the father's friends and relatives. They all protested vigorously at this poor, innocent father being put in prison. Confucius explained his reasons for doing so.

'When parents and elders fail to teach their young to love and treat others with respect and decency, why then should they bring them to me for punishment? The responsibility for the behaviour of our young rests firstly with the parents and supported by adults in general.'

Both father and son were released.

Confucius says so eloquently what I feel so deeply about our children. They are OUR children wherever they are, whoever they are; whatever their parents have done or not done. It is as simple as that.

Our young know little of the teachers or philosophers of the past. Sadly, with the break-up in family life they don't even have grandparents to guide, confide in or generally be there for them. Grandparents had a very special place within the family. Grandma was the one person who "never told" or betrayed a confidence.

As a grandmother, I feel so concerned at the plight of the world's children. The breakdown in family life to which Dr Fisher, the former Archbishop of Canterbury, referred a long time ago, has not been taken seriously. Children only learn within a loving, secure and disciplined family unit preferably with two loving adults. If they aren't shown love how can they learn to love? Adults teach children to love. They also teach them to hate.

The divorce rate continues to rise and more and more inadequate people produce unwanted children – people who cannot provide even the most basic home for their offspring. Some are little more than children themselves. I feel they put the cart before the horse. Generally speaking, in the animal world a "home" is carefully created by both male and female before the young arrive and they arrive at a time when food is at its most plentiful. We have all witnessed the activities of the birds in the spring lovingly preparing their nests for their young. Why then do humans produce their young in such a cursory way? They frequently give little thought to where they will live, how their young will be fed and, unlike the animals and birds, expect others to accept this responsibility for them.

The church has done little to address this worldwide problem. The cardinal sin, as far as the church is concerned, is to have sex before marriage so great emphasis is placed on the marriage act. So long as couples are married they can do what they like. I would suggest that couples should live together, get to know each other – particularly each other's weaknesses – and when it is felt they can maintain a permanent, long term relationship where children will be loved, secure and disciplined, then and only then, make the marriage commitment, followed by a "planned" family. This is plain common sense. The most important undertaking that two people can make is a commitment to the family, for which there is no substitute.

★

I remember an American at a function attended by my husband and me introducing his wife to us and proudly saying, 'This is my wife number three.'

In conversation later in the evening he discovered my husband and I had been married for almost 45 years.

He remarked, 'Poor Andrew! Imagine being married to the same woman for 45 years.'

I doubt if he could have understood the following passage from *Adam Bede* by George Eliot:

'What greater thing is there for two human souls than to feel that they are joined for life – to strengthen each other in all labour, to rest on each other in all sorrow, to minister to each other in all pain, and to be with each other in silent, unspeakable memories?'

This, in my opinion, is what real love is all about.

★

The Life of Love

Feed the lamp with oil and let it not dim, and
Place it by you, so I can read with tears what
Your life with me has written upon your face.
Bring Autumn's wine. Let us drink and sing the
Song of remembrance to Spring's carefree sowing,
And Summer's watchful tending, and Autumn's
Reward in harvest.

Come close to me, oh beloved of my soul; the
Fire is cooling and fleeing under the ashes.
Embrace me, for I feel loneliness; the lamp is
Dim, and the wine which we pressed is closing
Our eyes. Let us look upon each other before
They are shut.

Kahlil Gibran

Jesus, our great teacher, asked us to love each other and to forgive our enemies. This is a very difficult thing to do but what is the point in perpetually fighting personal and past wars? Older people who were involved in the last war ought to set an example of love and forgiveness to the younger generation. Over the past 50 years the world has become a smaller place and it is wrong to harbour feelings of hatred towards the new generation of Germans and Japanese.

When my husband was a lad, he and five friends used to cycle at weekends during the summer holidays to a small seaside village on the south-west coast of Scotland. They had wonderful, carefree, camping weekends. Then war broke out and eventually they were all called up for service, my husband joining the Fleet Air Arm. He spent most of his service in Ceylon – now Sri Lanka. He was, sadly, the only one of the little camping group to survive the war. One of his friends was killed in Burma on the day the war ended. My husband went on to university to study engineering and his work eventually took him to Europe as well as Japan. He harbours no feeling of hatred for the Germans or Japanese and has spent many happy times with engineers from both countries. He feels that his young friends – in their late teens – were too intelligent and aware to expect him to spend 50 odd years filled with hatred seeking revenge for their deaths. They certainly would have expected him to offer the hand of friendship, love and forgiveness to their past enemies. A whole generation of young men in their late teens gave up their university places to fight for their country. They did this willingly to free Europe of tyranny in the belief that the world would be a better place, but, alas, this has remained a dream. There are people who are so spiritually immature that they cannot forgive. There are some who are still fighting the Battle of Bannockburn – as well as Culloden and the Boyne. We can only hope that such people will some day realise that the loving, forgiving way is the only way. As they grow and develop inwardly they will realise that this is correct.

On the other hand, we have people in our communities who do set a good example to our younger generation. One such person was the father in Northern Ireland who forgave the terrorists even when he had lost his daughter. He spent most of his years prior to his death trying to teach people to love and forgive. Listening to him on television, I felt he was one of nature's gentlemen and it is so sad he had to die before peace was established in Northern Ireland.

I talked frequently about the troubles in Northern Ireland with Kathleen, my lovely Irish friend who came to me on a daily basis to help generally in the house and with the children. My husband was away from home so much – like most engineers – when our children were small. I decided to put an advert in the newsagent's for help and Kathleen came to see me. As we sat chatting I could almost hear her thinking, 'She's a Scottish Presbyterian and I'm an Irish Catholic.' She became very guarded and decided to come for a month to see how things developed. She stayed for 35 years. We grew old and became pensioners together. She was the dearest person, outside my family, whom I've ever known. She was totally loyal and there was nothing that she didn't know about us. Can you imagine missing out on this rare, beautiful friendship because of a difference in religion? Sadly, she died last year and it was like losing a little bit of myself.

Once again, I return to conversation with my father as a child.

He told us, 'Never, never accept the opinions of others. You will not go far in life if you do so. Always think for yourself and form your own views.'

This is exactly what people in Northern Ireland – and elsewhere – ought to do. Why follow, like a crowd of sheep, ministers who set themselves up as leaders and possess neither love nor compassion? The only thing they possess in abundance is the "gift of the gab". They are sad, bigoted people who live in the past.

Can't ordinary folk stop, think and ask, 'What am I doing following such people? Is this hatred, bigotry and bitterness going to solve anything?'

★

Man's inhumanity to man makes countless thousands mourn.

Robert Burns

★

What is hateful to you, do not to your fellow men. That is the entire Law; all the rest is commentary.

Jewish Spirituality.

★

I remember my father telling me that life was a voyage and I was the captain of my ship. As I sailed through life I would be buffeted this way and that. There would be many tears and much laughter but, if I kept my ship on the correct course, I would sail into port and home much wiser. I must not allow anyone else to captain my ship and relegate me to first mate.

I would advise our young to think for themselves, trust no one 100 per cent, read everything that will help them to grow inwardly, discuss widely and remember at the end of the day their most precious possessions will be their capacity to love unconditionally and their character which they and they alone create. This was my father's advice to me more than 60 years ago.

21

In the midst of all the troubles all over the world there was one great beacon of light – Nelson Mandela. What an example this lovely gentleman sets for all mankind. Imagine spending 27 years in prison and on release feeling no hatred or bitterness towards your former enemies. It takes a very remarkable person to suffer so much for so long and yet emerge full of love for his fellow men. He is my hero and it was particularly gratifying to hear him talk so lovingly and respectfully about our queen. It made a welcome change from the appalling abuse she has inflicted upon her by the press in her own country.

★

The soul has to learn to give love.
Love is an inward beauty which springs from the heart.

★

Hatred and bitterness can never cure the disease of fear;
only love can do that;
Hatred paralyses life; love releases it.
Hatred confuses life; love harmonises it.
Hatred darkens life; love illumines it.

Martin Luther King

★

We ought to Love and do good, not for the sake of reaping a reward, but because it is the beautiful, the fitting, the harmonious, the lawful thing to do. It is a fact that the great problems that face our society, greater now than ever before, cannot be solved by general laws but only through changes in attitudes to others.

Wilding

Love is the most universal, the most tremendous and the most mysterious of the cosmic forces.

Pierre Teilhard de Chardin

★

Love and you shall be loved. All love is mathematically just, as much as the two sides of an algebraic equation.

R.W. Emerson
Essay on Compensation

★

When we look back over life, the "big" moments don't come rushing back to give pleasurable memories but a few small acts of love and kindness from unexpected people in unexpected places seem to stand out beyond all others.

One such kindness springs immediately to my mind. My husband and I were told that there was a small nursery 20 kms from the village in which we were staying where it was possible to get seedlings for our garden. To get something to grow at all in a desert area always appeared to me a miracle but we decided we would make the journey and set off on a Saturday morning.

We found the nursery and in the shade of a lorry sat five men – powwow fashion. When they saw us approaching one got up and came towards us. He shook my husband by the hand but didn't ask what we wanted nor were we told we were trespassing. However, in perfect English, he asked if we would like to join them for lunch. To be shown such love and kindness by total strangers in such a lonely, deserted place, was a really beautiful experience. We were allowed to take as many seedlings as we wanted. We have so much to learn from people considered "primitive" and I would say to them, 'Stay as sweet as you are and don't let the world ever change you.'

★

A Moslem Prayer

LORD:
take away my conceit and give me confidence;
remove my doubts and give me faith;
give me strength over myself but do not give me strength
over others;
make me overcome my desires and reduce my wants;
let me not make fun of failures nor tread on the defeated;
help me to assist those who have fallen by the wayside;
fill my heart with mercy and remove all despotism;
let me judge myself before judging others;
make me able to see my faults and sins;
cover the eye that registers other people's faults;
do not stand by me when I am unfair but be with me only
when I am treated unfairly;
let me not regret that I loved but make me sad that I did
not love all people
always remind me of your grace and let me not forget
your blessings;
let me remember the favours of my helpers and the rights
of those who taught me;
let me forget those who forsake me;
remove the desire to punish but grant me the ability to do
favours;
close my heart to malice and envy and open it to let love
and forgiveness flow;
help me to make the largest number of people happy;
happy eyes are the lanterns that send away darkness.

To love and simply care about others was mentioned so often
n Robert Burns's poetry. He loved Scotland and its culture but
e was "no wee Scotlander". On the contrary, he was a great
nternationalist and when he wrote, "A Man's a Man for A'
hat", it was thought of as an "Anthem for the world". He
erived his inspiration from "brotherly love":

hen let us pray that come it may,
s come it will for a' that,
hat sense and worth o'er a' the earth.
May bear the gree and a' that,
or a' that, and a' that,
's coming yet, for a' that,
hat man to man, the world o'er,
hall brithers be for a' that.

May bear the gree = May win the victory)

This was written away back in the eighteenth century an
Robert Burns is known all over the world for his lovin
protest for the dignity of all humanity. Like Martin Luthe
King, he was shown little love or compassion by the establish
ment during his life but, also like Martin Luther King, he had
"dream" that men all over the world would learn to love an
respect each other as members of the human family irrespectiv
of class, creed or colour.

★

> I sought my soul but my soul I could not see,
> I sought my God but my God eluded me,
> I sought my brother and found all three.

★

Love is of the spirit and by it you recognise the spirit in
your brother or sister no matter how deceptive appear-
ances are.

Martin Luther Kin

★

Martin Luther King argues that we can all be great becaus
everyone can serve. You don't have to have a college degree t
serve. You don't have to make your subject and verb agree t
serve. You don't have to know about Plato and Aristotle to serv
You don't have to know about Einstein's theory to serve. Yo
only need a heart full of grace and a soul generated by love.

★

Greatness, after all, in spite of its name, appears to be, not
so much a certain size as a certain quality in human lives.

Phillip Brook

26

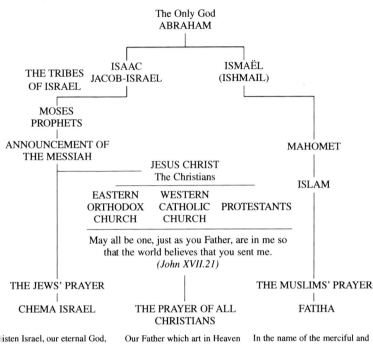

The Only God
ABRAHAM

THE TRIBES OF ISRAEL — ISAAC JACOB-ISRAEL — ISMAËL (ISHMAIL)

MOSES
PROPHETS

ANNOUNCEMENT OF THE MESSIAH

JESUS CHRIST
The Christians

MAHOMET

ISLAM

EASTERN ORTHODOX CHURCH — WESTERN CATHOLIC CHURCH — PROTESTANTS

May all be one, just as you Father, are in me so
that the world believes that you sent me.
(John XVII.21)

THE JEWS' PRAYER

CHEMA ISRAEL

THE PRAYER OF ALL CHRISTIANS

THE MUSLIMS' PRAYER

FATIHA

isten Israel, our eternal God,
ιe Eternal is one,
  he blessed? The glory of his
eign is eternal.
ou will love your eternal God
/ith all your heart, with all your
ιul and with all your will.
ιay the works which I set down
·day be engraved on your heart.
ιou will teach them to your
ιildren,
ιou will speak them in your
ιuse,
  hile going about your business,
ι rising and on going to bed.
·int them on your arm, engrave
ιem between your eyes, write
ιem on the beams of your
ιuse and on your doors.
ιou will remember all the
ιmmandments of the Lord in
·der to achieve them and
ιu will not follow the guilty
ιmptations of the eyes and
· the heart.

Our Father which art in Heaven
Hallowed be thy name.
Thy Kingdom come,
Thy will be done
On Earth as it is in Heaven.
Give us this day our daily bread,
Forgive us our trespasses
As we forgive those who
trespass against us.
Lead us not into temptation
But deliver us from evil.

In the name of the merciful and
compassionate God,
infinitely good and merciful.
Praise be to God, Lord of the
Universe.
Infinitely good and merciful.
Sovereign of the day of
Judgement
it is you alone whom we adore.
You alone whose help we seek.
Guide us in the right path
The path of those on whom
you have bestowed your benefits,
not the path of those who
have been the object of
your anger; nor of those
who have lost their way.
Amen.

*I photographed the above "Family Tree" in a church in Vernon
on my way to Giverny. It illustrates beautifully the meaning of
"The Brotherhood of Man". Many thanks to Mr John M. Grey
for his translation from the French.*

27

The greatest service anyone can give is to continually think aright, to love and forgive.

★

Where there is faith there is love,
Where there is love there is peace,
Where there is peace there is God,
Where there is God there is no need.

★

Love is strong, love is true, love is wise, love is tolerant, love is the divine solvent of every pain and every problem.

★

Love is seeing good, seeing God, recognising the divine law of cause and effect working throughout all life. To love is to be tolerant towards all men, towards all the happenings of daily life; to be patient, thoughtful kind and meek. All these qualities are contained in the one word love.

★

Can you imagine a world where we were all alike; all th same colour following the same religion or philosophy? Differences in religion, culture and appearance make people inter esting.

★

Like the bee gathering honey from different flowers, the wise man accepts the essence of different scriptures and sees only the good in all religions.

Rabindranath Tago

★

The mind boggles at the power of love. Imagine – if people who perpetually yearn for powerful positions all over the world were gifted with the power of love, the power to care about *all* people everywhere instead of their own little selves and the band of tiny people who make up their world. It is true that the higher a man's intellect the less intelligent, aware and loving he appears to be.

★

Slavery to intellect is the curse of our age.

Canon Pearce-Higgins

★

Ignorance is the curse of God; knowledge the wing wherewith we fly to Heaven.

William Shakespeare
Henry VI Part 2

★

As man is to the animal in the slowness of his evolution so is the spiritual man to the natural man.

Henry Drummond

★

We are just beginning to realise that we have a duty to the entire human family since we are all members one of another – even a duty and awareness that our planet and all living creatures must be treated with love and reverence – 'reverence for life', to quote Albert Schweitzer. To concern ourselves

30

with the destruction of rain forests and ozone layers and "green" issues in general will solve absolutely nothing if we have not learnt to love one another. This love and awareness are so slow in developing that one despairs at the future which awaits our grandchildren. But how do we become more aware? How do we develop the love and awareness of the teachers of the past? Do we develop awareness in childhood by example?

★

> I, that still pray at morning and at eve,
> Loving those roots that feed us from the past,
> And prizing more than Plato, things I learned,
> At that best Academe, a mother's knee,
> Thrice in my life perhaps have truly prayed,
> Thrice stirred below my conscious self, have felt
> That perfect disenthralment which is God.

J.R. Lowell
from *The Cathedral*

★

Do consciously what the flowers do unconsciously – "GROW".

Goethe

★

Our main aim in life should be 'how better we can love'. It is not an easy task!

Henry Drummond

★

We all know that a young person can be more sensitive, loving and aware than an elderly person who has lived a lifetime and is as ignorant as the day she was born.

This is the true story of a little boy called Jonathan who had a very severe stammer and was asked by his teacher to stand up and read to the whole class. This request caused not only him but his friend, Andrew, a great deal of distress. That evening Andrew was heard by his mother sobbing and crying in bed. When asked the cause of his distress he related the above incident, adding that Jonathan's face got redder and redder as he tried so bravely not to cry as some boys tittered and laughed. This story demonstrates that the little boy of nine, who felt so deeply for his friend, was blessed with more awareness than his "teacher" who was in her fifties and completely unaware of the turmoil her insensitive behaviour had caused. It is quite wrong to equate wisdom with age.

★

Lord, help me to see the world from other people's viewpoint not just my own. Show me what my thoughtlessness can do to them. Give me the tact that springs from love.

★

Some of us find it difficult to understand how human beings can be filled with hatred because someone is coloured, belongs to a different religion or is in some way handicapped and a little "different" from their idea of "normal". Such ignorance is unbelievable but it is the norm rather than the exception.

I remember being told by my father that we must not fall into the trap of believing we were "educated" unless we could walk through the front door out into the world and identify with anyone we met no matter who they were or where they came from. Religion, class, colour or handicap were unimportant. All the degrees in the world were useless, he said, if we could not do this very simple thing.

In the World Games in 1991 the final event brought a gold medal. There we had team work – black and white together – and the result was "golden". A golden future would surely await our children and grandchildren if only we could learn to love each other and work as a team to bring about a more loving, tolerant and peaceful world.

★

True happiness is only attainable when
we have learnt to love all people.

★

Individuals have not started living until
they can rise above the narrow confines of their
individualistic concerns to the broader
concerns of all humanity whom they must love.

Martin Luther King

★

In *Symposium*, Plato said,

'Love, Eros, makes his home in men's hearts, but not in every heart, for where there is hardness he departs. His greatest glory is that he cannot do wrong nor does he allow it. All men serve him of their own free will. He who is not touched by love walks in darkness.'

★

No worse fate can befall a man in this world
than to live and grow old, alone and unloved.

Henry Drummond

★

He that loveth not knoweth not God; for God is love.

1 John IV

★

Love is infallible; it has no errors, for all errors are the want of love.

William Law

★

God forces no one, for love cannot compel, and God's service, therefore, is a thing of perfect freedom.

Hans Denk

★

34

The Way of Happiness

Keep your heart free from hate,
Your mind free from worry,
Live simply, expect little and give much,
Fill your life with love,
Scatter as much sunshine as you can,
Forget self and think of others.
Simply: do as you would be done by.

★

Love some one – in God's name
love some one – for this is
the bread of the inner life, without
which a part of you will
starve and die; and though you
feel you must be stern,
even hard, in your life of affairs,
make for yourself at least
a little corner, somewhere in the
great world, where you may
unbosom and be kind.

Max Ehrmann

★

Give me a pure heart that I may see Thee,
A humble heart that I may hear Thee,
A heart of love that I may serve Thee,
A heart of faith that I may abide in Thee.

Dag Hammarskjöld

Work is love made visible. And if you cannot work with love but only with distaste, it is better that you should leave your work and sit at the gate of the temple and take alms of those who work with joy.

Kahlil Gibran

★

The Mosque at Marsa el Brega. We watched this lovely little Mosque grow out of the sand. Eventually, standing at the door of our house, we could see the dome and minaret slowly appear over the rooftops of the bungalows opposite.

Love is the greatest thing in the world.

★

Paul said, 'If I have all faith so that I can remove mountains and have not love, I am nothing'.

★

Peter said, 'Above all things have fervent love among yourselves'.

★

John went further and said, 'God is love'.

★

Paul said,
'If I speak with the tongues of men and of angels, and have not love, I am become as sounding brass or a tinkling cymbal'.
We have all experienced people talking so eloquently without any emotion, their words so insincere, but the speaker so persuasive. Eloquence, in other words, of politicians and others in high places who do not know the meaning of the word "love".

★

Love is life in its fullness, like the cup with its wine.

Rabindranath Tagore

★

The following passage was written by Henry Drummond, a Scottish scientist evangelist away back in 1883. He delivered his beautiful essay on love at a mission station in Central Africa. Unless we treat our world and all life in it with the greatest respect and teach our young accordingly, then his prophecy could well become a reality. It appears to me that the other important factor which we must all address sooner than later is the increase in world population. We ignore this at our peril as our planet cannot support uncontrolled increases in population forever.

'The words which all of us shall one day hear sound not of politics or theology, but of life; not of churches and saints but of the hungry and the poor; not of creeds and doctrines but of shelter and clothing; not of speeches, bibles or prayer books but of cups of cold water in the name of Christ. Who is Christ? He who fed the hungry, clothed the naked, visited the sick. Where is Christ? Who so shall receive a little child in my name receiveth Me. Who are Christ's? Everyone that loveth is born of God.'

We must learn to look at people and see them as members of the human family whom we must love. We must cease to categorise people by their religion or philosophy, by their colour, handicap or sexual orientation. All over the world we have one group fighting another. In Central Africa we have one tribe attempting to eliminate another. When Jesus, our great teacher, taught us to love He did not envisage any exceptions to His teaching. He did not mean love your neighbour – over the garden wall. Nor did He mean love only the people who attend your particular church. He meant love every member of the human family without exception.

I sometimes feel the Church is still in its infancy – it has still to grow up. God, to the Church, is a Father Christmas figure sitting up in the Heavens looking down on us all. I often wonder what the deprived, the homeless, the persecuted, the "little people" who are abused by the very adults who ought to protect them, think about such teaching. They must feel that this personal God preached about in Church has completely forgotten about them. One little boy was told by his teacher, rather curtly, that he hadn't listened to a word she had said all day. He related this to his grandma with whom he lived. She asked him why he'd been inattentive. He replied that he'd been "prayering and prayering" all day long that his mummy would come to the school gate to pick him up instead of her so that the children would all see he had a mummy just like them. The personal God preached about in church is of little comfort to children like this little boy. I wonder how many little ones lie in bed at night "prayering" just to be loved and wanted by their own parents.

I know how I felt when I was young and had to sit and listen to dreary sermons where love was never mentioned. I remember sitting thinking that when I reached 18 and left home I was going to "get out of this routine" and think for myself. I did and I haven't had any church experiences since that would make me believe that the decision I made 50 years ago was the wrong one. I was determined to do my own thinking and not accept other people's views – exactly as my father had taught me – and travel my own road.

I do not have hang-ups about colour or religion or different groups in our society. And why? It is quite simple. I refuse to accept other people's views and prejudices. My advice to our young would be to do the same. No wonder they look like wee boats sailing along without rudders with no idea where they are going. Role models are few and far between, with parents passing their responsibility to the teachers and others. The behaviour of politicians, church leaders, pop stars, footballers and others leaves much to be desired. Parents are particularly to blame and have little time for their children if they interfere with the type of life they want to live. The worst scenario is when they throw their children out and couldn't care less what happens to them.

There is a spiritual power that cannot be defined. This I have experienced for myself, as have so many others. The most beautiful moment in my life was when I realised that that which I could not see actually existed. We can call it "God" if we like but let no one believe that these beautiful, spiritual experiences belong only to one religion or one particular "God". Jesus was a wonderful teacher and left us a "spot on" recipe for living – that we should love one another. No other commandment is necessary. Keep this one commandment and we automatically fulfil the other ten.

To weave a lot of fantasy around Jesus and his life does Him the most incredible injustice. What misery and suffering there is in this world that is carried out in His name. It makes me cringe.

It has been my experience that the more "religious" people are the less loving and compassionate they appear to be.

It is my belief that the majority of church leaders don't even believe what they preach any more. This is nothing new. I recollect reading a biography of Jung (I can't remember the

40

author) in which it was mentioned that one of the saddest days in Jung's life was when he realised his elderly pastor father had spent his entire life teaching a belief he didn't accept himself. I can't imagine anything worse than spending a lifetime teaching a subject in which one didn't passionately believe.

When Dr David Jenkins, the former Bishop of Durham, tried to bring the Church into the twentieth century he became so unpopular and was widely abused. He was even blamed for the fire at York Cathedral – it was God's wrath for his utterings. Such thinking borders on the absurd.

Other religions and philosophies are equally to blame. I remember walking to school when I lived on the edge of the desert and being surrounded by four or five small children – three-year-olds. They prodded me and pointed upwards shouting 'Allah', smiled and displayed praying hands. They prodded me again pointing downwards to the ground and they all spat. Their message was loud and clear. I realised it would take generations to free people from this sort of bigotry when even small children were being taught to hate instead of love.

Anne, my lovely next door neighbour, is a Roman Catholic. We look after each other's houses when away and chat about our gardens and grandchildren. Imagine, if suddenly religious hatred made such friendliness impossible and we started throwing bricks at each other's windows or, in fact, worse. It sounds preposterous but I'm afraid it is not. This is exactly what is happening amongst people who have lived together for decades. It is not only peculiar to Northern Ireland. It is happening all over the world.

★

The Buddha, Mohammed, Confucius and many more lived and taught like Jesus. Their teachings are so beautiful and very similar, with love as their theme. Man's interpretations are the big problem. These wonderful verses from the *Bhagavad-Gita* provide so much food for thought:

When goodness grows weak and evil increases
I make myself a body,
In every age I come back,
To deliver the holy,
To destroy the sin of the sinner,
To establish righteousness.

Whatever wish men bring to me in worship,
That wish I grant them,
Whatever path men travel,
Is my path,
No matter where they walk.
It leads to me.

★

People of Orphalese, of what can I speak save of that which is even now moving within your souls.

Then said Almitra 'Speak to us of Love'.

And he raised his head and looked upon the people, and there fell a stillness upon them. And with a great voice he said:

When love beckons to you, follow him,
Though his ways are hard and steep.
And when his wings enfold you yield to him,
Though the sword hidden among his pinions may wound you.
And when he speaks to you believe in him,
Though his voice may shatter your dreams as the north wind lays waste the garden.

For even as love crowns you so shall he crucify you.
Even as he is for your growth so is he for your pruning.
Even as he ascends to your height and caresses your tenderest branches that quiver in the sun,
So shall he descend to your roots and shake them in their clinging to the earth.
Like sheaves of corn he gathers you unto himself.
He threshes you to make you naked.
He sifts you to free you from your husks.
He grinds you to whiteness.
He kneads you until you are pliant;
And then he assigns you to his sacred fire, that you may become sacred bread for God's sacred feast.

All these things shall love do unto you that you may know the secrets of your heart, and in that knowledge become a fragment of Life's heart.

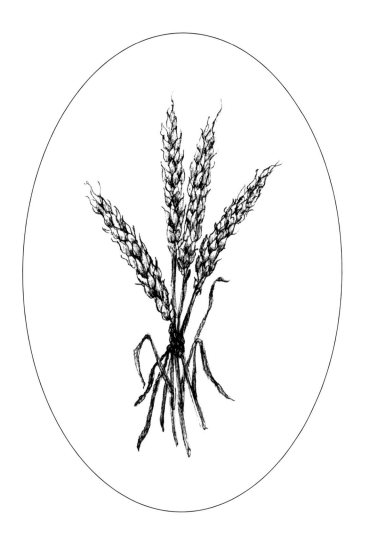

But if in your fear you would seek only love's peace and love's pleasure,
Then it is better for you that you cover your nakedness and pass out of love's threshing-floor,
Into the seasonless world where you shall laugh, but not all of your laughter, and weep, but not all of your tears.

Love gives naught but itself and takes naught but from itself.
Love possesses not nor would it be possessed;
For Love is sufficient unto love.

When you love you should not say, 'God is in my heart', but rather, 'I am in the heart of God.'
And think not you can direct the course of love, for love, if it finds you worthy, directs your course.
Love has no other desire but to fulfil itself.
But if you love and must needs have desires, let these be your desires:

To melt and be like a running brook that sings its melody to the night.
To know the pain of too much tenderness.
To be wounded by your own understanding of love;
And to bleed willingly and joyfully.
To wake at dawn with a winged heart and give thanks for another day of loving;
To rest at the noon hour and meditate love's ecstasy;
To return home at eventide with gratitude;
And then to sleep with a prayer for the beloved in your heart and a song of praise upon your lips.

from *The Prophet* by Kahlil Gibran

★

Children must be taught to love nature – the flowers, the birds, the animals and everything around them. It is so important to start educating them as early as possible in this way. As children, we knew the names of all the birds, the wild flowers and trees. We could even identify birds' eggs.

I was brought up in a house literally at the bottom of the most wonderful glen with a burn running through it in which I played. We lived there for many years until we moved to a more convenient house as we grew older. In my mind's eye I can still picture the scenes of my early childhood – they were magical. There was a meadow across the road from our home and in the spring it was a mass of beautiful wild flowers. I remember, when I was about three years old, wandering out of the gate, across the road and lying down in this "wild garden". I could hear my mother calling for me but pretended I didn't hear her. Eventually, I got up and ran home. It is, possibly my earliest memory and is still magic to me. My love of flowers, I feel started there and Kahlil's "Song of the Flowers" never fails to reduce me to tears, as does so much of his beautiful writing. It is so difficult to believe that he wrote most of my favourite pieces when he wasn't yet 20.

47

The Song of the Flower

I am a kind word uttered and repeated
By the voice of Nature;
I am a star fallen from the
Blue tent upon the green carpet.
I am the daughter of the elements
With whom Winter conceived;
To whom Spring gave birth; I was
Reared in the lap of Summer and
Slept in the bed of Autumn.
At dawn I unite with the breeze
To announce the coming of light;
At eventide I join the birds
In bidding the light farewell.

The plains are decorated with
My beautiful colours, and the air
Is scented with my fragrance.

As I embrace Slumber the eyes of
Night watch over me, and as I
Awaken I stare at the sun, which is
The only eye of the day.

I drink dew for wine, and harken to
The voices of the birds, and dance
To the rhythmic swaying of the grass.

I am the lover's gift; I am the wedding wreath;
I am the memory of a moment of happiness;
I am the last gift of the living to the dead;
I am a part of joy and a part of sorrow;
But I look up high to see only the light.
And never look down to see my shadow.

This is wisdom which man must learn.

Jung was right when he said,
'The thing that man has most to fear is man himself.
He is the origin of all past and coming evil.'

★

In other living creatures ignorance of self is nature – in man it is vice.

Boëthius

★

Fruitless is the wisdom of him who has no knowledge of self.

R.W. Emerson

★

Time is:
Too slow for those who wait;
Too swift for those who fear;
Too long for those who grieve;
Too short for those who rejoice;
But –
for those who love
Time is eternity.

Henry van Dyke

★

50

Some years ago, prior to Christmas, my husband and I decided to do some last minute shopping. It was a "late night" shopping evening in town and we came to a church where a carol service was in progress. We wandered in and found the place packed and were led to seats at the back which weren't normally used by the congregation. There was a lovely atmosphere but this was short-lived. An old, homeless gentleman wandered in carrying his paper bag with bottles clinking and, like ourselves, looked around for somewhere to sit. We moved along our seat to make room for him.

Before he could sit down, however, he was grabbed by a warden and told, 'This is no place for you. Come along. Out'.

We tried to tell the warden that there was room for him to sit down but to no avail. Our whole evening was spoilt by that one unloving, uncharitable act. I shall never forget it nor the smugness and superiority of everyone around.

'Father forgive them, for they know not what they do.'

★

We hand folks over to God's mercy and show none ourselves.

George Eliot
from *Adam Bede*

Man's bitter travail, his evolution, his progress, will bring him some day to the time when there will be but one brotherly thought prevailing, one pure harmony, one selfless desire and pure love abroad in the world. Never, never will man be established in aught but his own sorrow so long as he seeks for personal gain or supremacy. Only one true religion exists, only one reality behind all form, belief, sect, creed and ceremony. This is a universal religion, neither bound nor circumscribed by geographical limitations, convention or prejudice. It has but one name. That name can be understood by any man – black or white – as well as by animal and bird, by tree and flower, and every living creature instinct with the breath of life. The religion of true brotherhood has but one meaning and that is "love".

From *The Return of Arthur Conan Doyle*

★

We must love one another or die.

W.H. Auden

To love was Jesus's only commandment. I hope that as we reach the millennium more emphasis will be placed on "Jesus the Teacher" and less surrounding his mythical birth and death. The aim of each one of us as the millennium approaches is surely, "How better we can love". Love brings such happiness to the giver and renews faith and confidence in the receiver.

To quote Victor Hugo 'The supreme happiness of life is the conviction that we are loved.'

Our task is to try to change the way people think, as pushing new bills through Parliament will not solve anything or make the world more loving, beautiful and peaceful for our children.

Love is all we need.